TABLE OF CONTENTS

4

ABOUT YOUR ADVENTURE

You are living through the massive conflict that is World War I. You have chosen to serve your country as a spy. That means using secret codes, wearing disguises, gathering information—and trying not to get caught.

In this book you'll explore how the choices people made meant the difference between life and death. The events you'll experience happened to real people.

Chapter One sets the scene. Then you choose which path to read. Follow the directions at the bottom of each page. The choices you make will change your outcome. After you finish your path, go back and read the others for new perspectives and more adventures.

YOU CHOOSE the path
you take through history.

The assassination of Archduke Franz Ferdinand of Austria and his wife, Sophie, started a rapid chain of events that led to war.

WORLD AT WAR

You are living during a time of great conflict around the world. More than a dozen countries and their colonies have taken sides in a war that began in Europe in July 1914. People are calling this conflict the Great War.

Austria-Hungary declared war on Serbia after Austrian Archduke Franz Ferdinand was killed. A Bosnian Serb assassin killed Ferdinand and his wife on June 28 in the city of Sarajevo, Bosnia-Herzegovina. Bosnia-Herzegovina is ruled by Austria-Hungary, but some Serbs living there want their independence. After Ferdinand's murder Austria claimed the assassin had help from neighboring Serbia, Austria's rival.

7

TURN THE PAGE.

Both Serbia and Austria-Hungary have allies in Europe. Serbia's main support comes from the Allied Powers, including Russia, France, and the United Kingdom. Together those three nations form what is called the Entente. Austria's main allies are Germany and the Ottoman Empire, which stretches almost to North Africa and across the Middle East. These countries form the core of the Central Powers. Other countries around the world also support one side or the other, though not all send troops into battle.

The United States, though, has not entered the war. President Woodrow Wilson said the country would remain neutral. Still, many Americans, including Wilson, support the British and their allies. At the same time, several million German Americans have strong feelings for their homeland.

Even before the war, European countries conducted espionage against one another. They sent agents to gather intelligence or sought out people who might be willing to give them information. Many countries also developed agencies to carry out counterespionage.

TURN THE PAGE.

After Austria-Hungary declared war on Serbia on July 28, 1914, Serbian troops marched to the border to defend against invasion.

You have read about spies and the work they do both before and during wars. The life of a spy seems exciting, although you realize it can also be very dangerous. Spies who are caught risk going to prison or being killed by their country's enemies. Still, you want to do what you can to help your country during this growing world war. And spying is how you'll do it.

11

TO BE A GERMAN SPY, TURN TO PAGE 13.

TO BE A FEMALE BELGIAN SPY, TURN TO PAGE 43.

TO BE A BRITISH SPY WORKING IN RUSSIA, TURN TO PAGE 71.

Many Germans gathered in cities such as Berlin to show their support for the war effort.

CHAPTER 2

SPYING FOR THE FATHERLAND

"I must do something for the Fatherland!"

"But you've already served in the military," says your mother, surprised. "Why do you want to get involved with this war?"

You returned to Germany, your "Fatherland," earlier in 1914. Now the Great War has begun. You had lived in America since a visit years ago led to you marrying an American woman. But when you recently divorced, you decided to go back to Germany. Now, as Germany battles the United Kingdom, you imagine using your fluent English to spy on the British.

13

TURN THE PAGE.

You decide it would be best to keep quiet about your plan. The next day you take a train to Berlin. You find your way to Abteilung IIIB, the government's top military intelligence agency. You meet an officer named Captain Imhoff. You explain that you had served in the Navy reserve before and want to serve as a spy. You also tell him about your language skills.

"It's very brave to volunteer," Imhoff says. "But we don't have much time to train you."

"I don't care," you say. "I'm ready."

"Perhaps you would prefer to work for naval intelligence." Imhoff suggests. "It would make sense because of your naval experience. But we also need agents who speak with American accents."

You sound like a native-born American after living in the United States. You also know other Germans there who might be able to help you. But Imhoff is right—you already have a great knowledge of ships and sailors. The British navy is a major threat. And since it's much closer to Germany, you could get there faster and start spying sooner.

Britain used its powerful navy to set up a blockade to keep imported food and supplies from reaching Germany and Austria-Hungary.

TO WORK FOR NAVAL INTELLIGENCE, TURN TO PAGE 16.

TO PUT YOUR ACCENT TO WORK IN THE UNITED STATES, TURN TO PAGE 22.

Imhoff sends you to naval intelligence officers who give you the addresses of German agents you can contact when you have information. You also receive a supply of formalin. This liquid chemical is mixed with lemon juice to create an invisible ink. The ink can be read when it's heated.

Next you travel to the U.S. Embassy in Berlin to get a fake U.S. passport. You think about the penalties for being caught as a spy—prison, or perhaps even death. Your heart pounds as you walk up to the counter.

"My name is Edward Reynolds," you say. "I'm a salesman from Boston doing business here in Germany. I lost my passport and need another so I can return home."

The clerk asks, "Do you have any other papers for identification?"

"Just a driver's license, but I left it in Boston."

The clerk looks at you, as if trying to see if you're telling the truth. Finally, he hands you a form and tells you to fill it out. Soon, you have a passport with your new name. You travel to London where you rent a small room. You tell the people you meet you're an American doing business in Europe.

You begin to travel to nearby port cities. You watch for soldiers boarding ships and try to learn where they are going and when they're leaving. Then you go back to your room and write to Hans Schmidt, your contact in Rotterdam, Netherlands. In normal black ink you write about an order for a fake business deal. In between the lines, you use your invisible ink to report the information you've gathered. Schmidt will then send the information to Berlin.

TURN THE PAGE.

One day you return to your room and see some of your neighbors whispering. They stop talking when they see you approach.

"Coming back from another business trip?" an elderly woman named Mrs. Smith asks.

"That's right," you say.

"You travel often, Mr. Reynolds," a man named Harris says.

You try to smile. But you have a bad feeling—your neighbors seem suspicious. You wonder if you should go to another city. Schmidt said naval intelligence would like to know more about ships sailing from Scotland. There is also an open assignment spying on the Harwich Force, a major British naval fleet in Harwich, northeast of London.

18

TO GO TO HARWICH,
GO TO PAGE 19.

TO GO TO SCOTLAND,
TURN TO PAGE 20.

You rent a room in Harwich and spend time near the docks. You use binoculars to look at the British ships as they return to port. You can see that one is so badly damaged it has to be towed. You plan to come back to Harwich over the next few weeks and see if it is being repaired.

As you leave the docks, you hear a voice behind you calling out. "You there!"

You turn and see a military police officer. Panic rises in your throat. Surely the officer will wonder why an American businessman is watching naval ships. But it will be worse if he finds the binoculars in your pocket. If you run you might get away, but the officer will know for sure you were up to something. If you stay maybe you can convince him your cover is real.

19

TO STAY,
TURN TO PAGE 29.

TO RUN,
TURN TO PAGE 31.

Late that night you pack up your belongings
and slip out of the boarding house. You travel to
Edinburgh, Scotland's capital. Not far away is
the Rosyth Royal Dockyard. Ships are repaired
and supplied there. Other naval ships are based
in the region.

*German submarines, called U-boats, placed explosive mines
in the water to blow holes in Allied ships.*

In Edinburgh, you hunt for more information about the nearby ships. You learn what you can from dock workers. They think you're just an innocent American salesman. You seem to win them over when you say, "I hope America joins the war to help fight those dirty Huns."

One day you read in the paper that the British have found a German spy guilty of "war treason." You realize that the man, named Lody, has a similar story to yours. Like you, he had been spying for German naval intelligence. The British are going to execute him for his espionage.

Sweat breaks out on your face and your hands **21** turn clammy. You wonder if it's safe to stay in England. The intelligence officers in Germany must be worried too. You soon receive word to go back to Berlin and see Imhoff. He wants you to go to the United States.

TURN TO PAGE 22.

Imhoff explains that Johann von Bernstorff has just been sent to the United States to lead Germany's spy efforts. His first goal is to try to keep the United States from entering the war against Germany. The other is to keep U.S. weapons and supplies from reaching the Allies. Imhoff wants you to help with the second goal.

"Von Bernstorff already has men working on the docks," he tells you. "They have plenty of money from our government to hire others to help plant bombs."

You travel to Hoboken, New Jersey. The city is full of German Americans as well as German sailors whose ships were forced to stay in U.S. ports once the war started. Even if they were allowed to set sail, it would be hard to reach Germany again. The British navy has put a blockade around the country.

After your arrival you go to meet your contact, Erich Strauss. He works for von Bernstorff, hiring men who work on the New York docks.

"We have a lot to do here," he says. "Ships leave every day to bring supplies to our enemies. We must stop them."

Strauss offers you the choice between two jobs. One is to stay in the city and work with men who place bombs in ships. The other is to take on a new mission, carrying out sabotage in Canada.

You would like to stay close to New York, a city you know well. And you're comfortable working around ships after your days in the Navy. But the idea of doing a different kind of sabotage is exciting. You feel good that Strauss trusts you to carry it out.

23

TO TAKE THE CANADIAN MISSION, TURN TO PAGE 24.

TO STAY IN NEW YORK, TURN TO PAGE 26.

Strauss outlines the plan. "We want you to blow up the Welland Canal between Lakes Ontario and Erie in Ontario. Canadian ships use the canal to bring raw materials to the United States. American factories turn those materials into weapons used against our soldiers."

Soon you are on a train to Niagara Falls on the U.S.-Canadian border. Under your seat is a suitcase filled with dynamite that Strauss bought for you. With you are some German sailors Strauss found. They volunteered to join the mission and help the Fatherland.

You stash the dynamite in a hotel on the U.S. side of the border. Then you go to the canal, which is visible from New York. You are shocked when you peer through your binoculars. There are soldiers guarding the waterway. You expected guards, but not so many well-armed soldiers.

"How many guards are there?" asks a sailor named Holtz.

"A lot," you reply. "Maybe hundreds."

Holtz shakes his head. "It's too dangerous."

The other sailors nod in agreement.

"Don't tell me you're cowards," you hiss.

"But we didn't plan for this," Holtz replies. "It would be suicide to try to get the dynamite to the canal with so many guards."

You look through the binoculars again. Maybe Holtz is right. Perhaps you should just go back to New York and tell Strauss the plan was impossible. If he's not upset, you could still plant bombs in New York.

25

TO CONTINUE THE MISSION,
TURN TO PAGE 33.

TO RETURN TO NEW YORK,
TURN TO PAGE 35.

Strauss gives you money and tells you to hire dock workers to plant bombs in ships. You hire some German Americans who work for German shipping companies. They are eager to help the Fatherland. Others are Irish who hate the British because they won't grant Ireland its independence. You also go to factories and pay workers $25 to plant bombs. Many are willing to risk being caught to earn that much money. It's as much as most of them earn in one week.

You watch the newspapers carefully. Several chemical plants have explosions and fires. So do ships heading for Europe. When you meet Strauss next, he's pleased with the sabotage.

"Now we have even bigger plans," he says. He explains that German leaders in Berlin want even more destruction. They want Strauss to arrange to blow up several munitions plants.

"Here is a list of some of the sites," he says. "And here is a list of other agents who can help."

You study the list of possible targets. The first two are Black Tom Island and Kingsland. Black Tom is a storage site for cannon shells and bullets waiting to be sent to Europe. Kingsland workers make shells that will go to Russia. Destroying either target will slow the delivery of munitions to Germany's enemies.

Spies were able to convince some dock workers to help sabotage Allied ships.

TO TRY TO BLOW UP BLACK TOM ISLAND, **TURN TO PAGE 38.**

TO TRY TO BLOW UP KINGSLAND, **TURN TO PAGE 28.**

"We have an agent already working there," Strauss says. "Perhaps he can help you and other agents get jobs too."

You leave Strauss and head back to Hoboken. After a while you notice two men in suits walking behind you. Are they following you? Now you begin to get nervous. Do they know Strauss is a German agent?

You put your hands in your jacket pockets and begin to walk faster. Then you realize that you still have the lists Strauss gave you. If you throw them away, the men tailing you might scoop them up. That might prove to them that you're an agent too. But if they decided to arrest you with the lists, that would be just as bad.

28

TO THROW OUT THE LISTS AND RUN, **TURN TO PAGE 40.**

TO KEEP WALKING NORMALLY, **TURN TO PAGE 41.**

You smile and approach the officer. "Is there a problem, sir?" you ask.

"What's your business here?" he asks.

You tell him your name and show him your passport. You explain that you're in England on business. "An old friend of mine used to live in Harwich. I'm trying to find his house, but I seem to have gotten lost," you say.

The officer looks at you sternly but lets you go without asking any more questions. You go back to your room to write to Schmidt. You tell him what you saw and that you plan to return to Harwich over the coming weeks.

29

Back in London you wait for a reply. After a few weeks Schmidt writes you with a surprising message—the officials in Berlin want you to come home!

TURN THE PAGE.

"Everything we receive from you is false or useless," Schmidt's letter reads. "Perhaps you are not meant to be a spy."

Then you realize what is happening. British censors read mail and telegrams sent overseas. They must have read your messages and found the invisible ink. Or maybe something else has tipped them off. But they are letting all your messages with false information go through. They must have pulled the letter about the damaged ship in Harwich. That explains why Schmidt never mentioned it. Now you just hope you can make it back to Rotterdam and then Germany without being caught.

THE
-END-

To follow another path, turn to page 11.
To read the conclusion, turn to page 101.

You sprint down the street. The officer blows his whistle, but no one is around to stop you. You speed ahead and lose him after ducking into an alley. You wait to catch your breath, then look both ways at the edge of the alley. No one is around. You head back to your room.

That night, as you leave the boarding house to get dinner, three men corner you. One of them is the military police officer from earlier today!

"That's him!" the officer says, pointing at you.

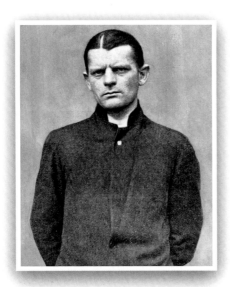

German naval reserve officer Carl Hans Lody was the first spy executed in Britain during World War I.

TURN THE PAGE.

"We're from the Secret Service," says one of the other men. "We've been following you for some time, Mr. Reynolds." You know the Secret Service handles counterespionage.

The officer makes you follow the two government agents inside. You feel doomed.

The men soon find your letter to Schmidt about what you saw today. They also see a lemon that you used to write in invisible ink. With a match, one of the agents lights a candle by your desk. When he puts the flame under the paper, the hidden message appears.

"You're under arrest for espionage," the other agent says. You know you will be brought to London and placed before a firing squad.

THE
-END-

To follow another path, turn to page 11.
To read the conclusion, turn to page 101.

"Let me cross to the Canadian side," you say. "Perhaps I can find a safer spot for the dynamite."

In Canada you take a closer look at the canal. After some exploration you discover a remote section that is not guarded. But when you return to the hotel to tell the others, the sailors are gone! Their fear must have led them to flee.

You return to New York City and tell Strauss what happened. He is angry with you.

"After this failure how can I trust you with anything important again?" he asks. "From now on you're going to be working on the ships."

33

Strauss sends you down to the docks with a new bomb. Shaped like a cigar, the metal device has acids inside of two separate copper chambers. The acids slowly break down the chambers and mix. When they combine they start a fire.

TURN THE PAGE.

Your job is to hide the cigar bomb in a ship carrying explosives to the Allies. The plan is to make a fire start while a ship is at sea. That way the Americans won't suspect that you or other dock workers planted the bombs.

You get a job loading explosives on a British ship. Below deck, where the cargo goes, no one is around. You carefully place bombs under the cargo as you load.

A few days later, Strauss comes over to you with a big smile.

"The bombs worked," he says. "The ship caught fire and all the explosives were destroyed."

You smile too. You're ready to plant more bombs to help Germany win the war.

THE
–END–

To follow another path, turn to page 11.
To read the conclusion, turn to page 101.

Strauss is angry at your failure and sends you back to Germany. But you feel better when you're given another mission. Captain Imhoff hands you a small black bag.

"Inside are germs that can kill horses," Imhoff says. "The Americans are shipping horses to the British and French to use on the battlefield."

Imhoff explains that your new mission is to bring the germs to America and use them to kill the horses before they reach the battlefield. He also wants you to go back in disguise.

"We hope the border guards will not be so suspicious of a woman," he says.

You set sail wearing women's clothing and a wig. The disguise seems to work well. You don't think anyone can tell you're really a man. You make it to New York without any problems.

TURN THE PAGE.

You spend the first few days exploring the docks and laying out a plan. Then, late one night, you go where the horses are kept. You take out a soft stick and a container of germ-filled liquid. You put liquid on the end of the stick. Then you swab the nearest horse's nose. The animal snorts and stomps. Your hands tremble but you try to keep steady as you repeat the procedure on more horses. Finally, you head back to your hotel.

During the war horses were essential for many tasks including hauling heavy weapons and supplies.

You read the newspaper every day, waiting to see a report about the dead horses. But nothing appears. Maybe you did something wrong. Or perhaps the germs had died before you could get to the horses. You panic—you've now failed on two missions. You decide you can't report back to Abteilung IIIB and continue as a spy. Instead, you return to Hoboken and try to blend in with the German Americans there.

You finally hear reports that some horses did get sick and die, but not as many as Imhoff had hoped. You didn't fail after all. Still, you're happy to be living in the United States with your risky days of spying behind you.

37

THE
-END-

To follow another path, turn to page 11.
To read the conclusion, turn to page 101.

A relative of your ex-wife, Carl Burg, works at Black Tom. He is an American citizen, but you sense he might like to see Germany win the war. You meet with Carl one day to see what you can learn about Black Tom Island.

"We're so busy," Carl says. "We can't load munitions on the ships quickly enough. The railroad cars sit there for days, full of explosives."

"There must be lots of security watching the munitions," you say casually. Carl explains that there are guards, but some areas of the site lack fences and are unlit.

You feel excitement rising in you. All this information will make Black Tom an easy target.

You meet Strauss and tell him all you learned. He tells you that Abteilung IIIB has brought in special agents to carry out the sabotage. In the meantime, he wants you to go back to the docks.

One morning a huge explosion wakes you. You rush outside to see bright lights streaking across the sky—right in the direction of Black Tom Island. The next day the newspaper reports that dozens of people were injured and buildings were destroyed for miles around. The sabotage was a success.

You continue your work on the docks. Strauss approves of your work. In January 1917 you read in the paper that the Kingsland factory was badly damaged by fire. You assume German agents carried that out as well. But in April the United States declares war on Germany. Many German agents begin fleeing to neutral Mexico. As you prepare to join them, you feel proud to have done your part to help Germany fight the Great War.

THE -END-

To follow another path, turn to page 11.
To read the conclusion, turn to page 101.

On a crowded spot on the street, you crumple and drop the papers, then duck into a hotel. You go through the hotel's basement and into a walkway leading to the subway. You board a train that will take you to the New Jersey ferry.

As you leave the dock in New Jersey, suddenly a hand grips you from behind.

"Hoboken police," the man says. "We got a call from the New York cops. Someone who looked a lot like you is suspected of spying for Germany. And the papers you dropped prove it."

40 You slump down to the ground. You can't lie anymore. You realize you will be arrested. You just hope that the Americans will send you back to Germany, rather than throw you in prison.

THE
-END-

To follow another path, turn to page 11.
To read the conclusion, turn to page 101.

You keep walking fast and then duck into an alley. Seconds pass, then a minute. The men do not appear.

When you get home, you memorize the list of agents and sabtoage sites, then burn the papers. You don't want to ever risk being caught with important information again. In the morning you meet Witt, the agent who works at Kingsland.

"It's no good," he tells you. "I can't get anyone a job now—I don't want to draw attention to myself. But don't worry, the plan will still go on." Months later you see that Witt was right when you read about a fire at the plant. You hope you will have a chance to carry out your own sabotage before the war ends.

41

THE
-END-

To follow another path, turn to page 11.
To read the conclusion, turn to page 101.

*German soldiers destroyed hundreds of
communities after invading Belgium.*

CHAPTER 3

THE WHITE LADY

In your dreams, you still see waves of German troops. They invaded your small town in Belgium three years ago, in 1914. But every day when you wake you see some of those same soldiers still walking the streets. The Germans now control most of the country. Every day they fight to take the rest of Belgium and capture France as well.

You and your friends and family are lucky. You didn't experience all the horrors other Belgians did. The Germans burned whole villages and killed innocent civilians. They have forced most men to leave their homes to work for the army. Belgian men like your father and your friends' fathers have been taken away to repair roads or make weapons.

43

TURN THE PAGE.

You and your mother struggle for food.
Most of what local farmers grow now goes to
the Germans. Their officers force you and other
nurses to treat the wounded. As you work,
you think how these soldiers have killed fellow
Belgians. You imagine how harshly the Germans
treat your father. And you hate how your country
and its people are being destroyed.

One evening, your best friend, Maria Heuven,
comes over and asks you to come outside.

*Many Belgians fled the invading Germans while
others hid in shelters to escape the violence.*

"My sisters and I are spying for the British," Maria whispers. "We have joined a secret group called La Dame Blanche—the White Lady."

Maria explains that a group of Belgians offered their services to the British. "We don't just send them information," Maria says. "We also help wounded soldiers and urge other Belgians to resist the Germans in any way they can."

"Isn't it dangerous?" you ask.

"Yes," she says. "But we're not alone. Even the local priests and nuns help us. Will you join too?"

You think about your father and wonder if you will ever see him again. Probably not, if the Germans win the war. You should try to help defeat them too. But if something happened to you, your mother would be alone. You don't know if she could survive.

45

TO SAY NO,
TURN TO PAGE 46.

TO SAY YES,
TURN TO PAGE 50.

"I'm sorry, Maria. I guess I'm just not as brave as you."

Maria simply nods, then returns home. You go inside hoping that Maria and her sisters are not caught.

A few days later, you go to the Heuvens' house. You haven't seen Maria since that night she came to see you.

"Where has she been?" you ask her sister Marthe.

"Did she tell you what we're doing?" Marthe asks. "About La Dame Blanche?"

Marthe goes on to explain that Maria volunteered to take messages to some agents in the Netherlands. They can work freely there, since that country is neutral.

"But she hasn't come back yet," Marthe says. "We haven't even had a message from her. We think she's been caught by the Germans."

You begin crying. You can only imagine what the Germans will do to her. You've heard that some female spies have been shot.

"Will you stop spying?" you ask.

Marthe shakes her head. "It's too important. And we all know the risks of doing what we do."

That night you imagine Maria under arrest, facing death. You decide you must take action to stop the Germans. In the morning you wake and run over to the Heuvens'. You tell Marthe you want to join La Dame Blanche. She hugs you then takes you to the home of the local leader of the group. You're surprised to see that it's Mrs. Van Vliet—one of the wealthiest people in town.

47

TURN THE PAGE.

Mrs. Van Vliet explains that many women hold important jobs in the group. "We are all united against the Germans," she says. "I'm glad you're willing to help. I have two possible assignments for you. One is to take messages to the Netherlands, as Maria did. The other is to spend time near the train station, to watch the movement of German trains."

Watching the trains sounds simple—and not too dangerous. But you like the idea of doing what Maria did, even if it is riskier.

48

TO WATCH THE TRAINS,
GO TO PAGE 49.

TO GO TO THE NETHERLANDS,
TURN TO PAGE 60.

Every day after work, you bike to the local train station. German trains pass through there on their way to the Western Front. They carry soldiers, horses, and weapons. You use a secret code Marthe gave you to write down how many of each you can see. You hide the paper inside the hollow handle of a basket tied to your bike. You then ride to a contact who works in a local shop and turn over the information you've gathered.

One evening you're riding home from the station. When you turn a corner, you see two German soldiers blocking the road. They signal for you to stop. You see an alley a few feet away. **49** You could ride into it and try to lose them in the dark. Or you can follow their orders and try your best to talk your way out of the situation.

TO KEEP RIDING, TURN TO PAGE 57.

TO STOP, TURN TO PAGE 58.

The next day, Marthe takes you to meet Mrs. Roenig. She comes from one of the wealthiest families in the village. You're proud to know that people of all backgrounds are helping to fight the Germans. Mrs. Roenig asks if you speak German.

"A little," you say. "And French too."

"You are just what the British are looking for," Mrs. Roenig says. She explains that she works with British intelligence agents in France. They are looking for new agents who speak both German and French.

"I want to sneak you out of Belgium and into France, so you can receive special training," says Mrs. Roenig. "The British will teach you how to use codes and write in invisible ink."

"Will it be safe for me to travel?" you ask.

"Nothing is safe for us these days. But we have members who will travel with you."

You want to do what you can to help La Dame Blanche. But you've never been away from home before. And you would have to tell your mother where you're going and why. She won't be happy to hear you want to become a spy.

Traveling Belgian civilians were in danger of being stopped and searched by German soldiers.

51

TO STAY HOME, TURN TO PAGE 52.

TO GO FOR THE TRAINING, TURN TO PAGE 54.

"Could I do something here?" you ask.

Marthe tells Mrs. Roenig that you are a nurse.

"That can be useful," Mrs. Roenig says. She asks you to talk to as many soldiers as you can. "Any information they tell you could be good. Then I'll make sure the British get it."

Normally, you don't talk to the German soldiers. But now you pretend to be their friend. The soldiers talk mostly about how much they hate the war. They miss their families and want to go home. But some also mention the movement of units from one Belgian town to another. Others talk about heading into France.

You write down the information as soon as you can, using a code that Mrs. Roenig taught you. You give the messages to Marthe or directly to Mrs. Roenig.

An officer named Colonel Heinz often stops by the hospital to ask about his men. One day he comes over to talk to you.

"Young lady, the soldiers say you take good care of them," he says. "Would you like to help us another way?" He explains that he works for German intelligence. "We have heard about a secret organization here in Belgium called La Dame Blanche. Have you heard about it?"

"No," you say, shaking your head.

Heinz asks if you will work for him, watching the activities of suspected spies. If you say yes, you'll become a double agent. You'll have to pretend to help Heinz while still working for La Dame Blanche. The Germans will surely kill you if they find out you're deceiving them.

53

TO BECOME A DOUBLE AGENT, **TURN TO PAGE 62.**

TO SAY NO, TURN TO PAGE 66.

You dread telling your mother you're leaving, but her reaction surprises you.

"I will miss you, sweetheart, but I will be all right," she says. "I'm proud that you are helping the Allies. And maybe you can learn something about your father."

Yes, through all this, you always think about your father. You think about him and all the other Belgians the Germans have dragged away and forced to work.

Within a few days, you are training with British intelligence agents in France. You impress them with your skill at learning codes and German military weapons. When you're ready to go home, the British instruct you to recruit others to work under you. You agree and soon your network is sending valuable information about German movements in Belgium.

You enjoy your work for La Dame Blanche. You feel excited when you send off a secret message written with invisible ink. But you try to be careful every day. You know that the Germans have agents trying to catch members of La Dame Blanche. And in return for money, some Belgians are surely willing to help the Germans.

One night after you leave the hospital, you go to see Marthe. When you go in, you notice that she looks upset. She motions her head to the side, and you see three German military police officers.

"You're under arrest," one says, and the men throw you and Marthe into a truck. You're taken to Germany, where you face a military trial.

55

"I should sentence you both to death," the judge says. "But instead you're going to Siegburg Prison."

TURN THE PAGE.

The prison holds other women arrested for spying. You and Marthe are shoved into tiny, cold cells. The Germans force you to make munitions. Some of the women don't like this, and Marthe suggests you all go on strike.

"Will you take part?" she asks you.

You don't like making munitions used to kill Allied troops. But if you go on strike, you could face even worse treatment from the guards.

When her hometown of Lille, France, was invaded by the Germans, Louise de Bettignies used her home to run a spy network to deliver information to the British.

TO GO ON STRIKE, TURN TO PAGE 65.

TO SAY NO, TURN TO PAGE 68.

You pedal hard and make a sharp turn down the alley. You hear the soldiers close behind, shouting for you to halt. You're almost at the end of the alley when you hear a gunshot, then another. Bullets whiz past above your head.

You've nearly escaped when a sudden jolt sends you flying headfirst over the bike's handlebars. There must have been a hole in the pavement, hidden in darkness. You come tumbling to a halt, hitting your head on something hard. Everything around you starts to spin and you can't move. Now the two Germans are standing above you, their guns pointing at your face. Just before passing out, you realize that you will be arrested. If you're lucky, you'll be sent to a German prison instead of being executed.

**THE
-END-**

To follow another path, turn to page 11.
To read the conclusion, turn to page 101.

57

You stop in front of the soldiers.

"Why are you out after dark?" one asks.

"I'm a nurse," you say, trying not to show your fear. "I had to stay late to treat a wounded soldier."

"We've heard reports that a young woman who looks likes you has been hanging around the train station," the soldier says.

"No, I'm never at the station," you lie.

"What's in the basket?" the other soldier asks.

"Nothing. I was just going to get some food at a friend's house." Before you can move, the soldier lunges at the basket and rips it off your bike. He pokes at it with his bayonet.

"There's something odd about this handle," he says. He smashes the handle with his gun and the paper with your coded notes falls out.

"You're a spy!" the first soldier says. "Who are you working with?"

"I'm not a spy!" you insist.

The second soldier points his gun at you. "Tell us or we will have your mother killed."

You gasp at this threat. When you joined La Dame Blanche, you promised never to reveal information about the group. But you can't bear the thought of losing your mother.

"All right," you say, hanging your head. "I'll tell you what I know."

59

You feel shame at betraying the members of La Dame Blanche. And you fear the prison that awaits you. But at least your mother will live.

THE -END-

To follow another path, turn to page 11.
To read the conclusion, turn to page 101.

"Marthe is going to the border tonight," Mrs. Van Vliet says. "You should go with her."

You agree and soon you and Marthe are riding your bikes toward the border. "How do you cross it?" you ask. "Aren't the Germans nearby?"

"Yes, but we have many ways of getting messages across," Marthe says. "Sometimes we bribe the guards. Other times we hide messages in beets or other foods and toss them over. But now things are more dangerous. The Germans have built an electric fence more than 9 feet tall between Belgium and the Netherlands."

You walk through an orchard and see the fence up ahead. You look around but don't see any German soldiers on the other side.

"Don't worry," Marthe says. "We won't cross tonight. We'll just throw some messages."

Marthe takes a beet out of her bike basket. She tosses it over the fence. From the other side comes the sound of a bird whistle. "That's the signal," Marthe says. "They found it." She hands you one. "You try."

You pull your arm back and then fling the beet. It doesn't clear the fence.

"I'll try again," you say, running toward the fence.

"Be careful!" Marthe warns.

You start to respond, but then you trip over a tree root sticking out of the ground. You stumble, lose your balance, and fall into the electric fence. With a flash of light, you die instantly.

61

THE
-END-

To follow another path, turn to page 11.
To read the conclusion, turn to page 101.

The colonel pulls out a list of names. "Do you know any of these people? They are suspected of trying to help the Allies."

He hands you the paper. You gasp when you see "Marthe Heuven" listed among the names. You glance at Heinz, but he doesn't seem to have noticed your reaction. After examining the paper, you tell Heinz that you don't know anyone listed.

"You must be careful," you tell Marthe that evening. "The Germans suspect you."

"But this is perfect," Marthe says. "All you have to do is wait a few days. Then tell the colonel you haven't seen me do anything suspicious."

You do as Marthe says. A few days later, you tell Heinz that Marthe and several others on the list are not spies. The colonel looks upset. "Can't you bring me anything useful?" he asks.

The next day, you meet Heinz after work. You hand him a rumpled bit of paper. "I found this by a dead pigeon," you say, knowing the Allies sometimes use trained pigeons to send secret messages. On the paper is a coded message— one that you made up yourself. The code is meaningless, but Heinz doesn't know this. He smiles when he sees it. "I will have our code breakers get to work on this right away!"

You worry a little. Could the code breakers figure out that the coded message is nonsense?

That evening you hear a buzzing sound overhead, followed by an explosion. Allied planes are attacking a German camp nearby! Airplanes were invented a little over 10 years ago, and already both sides are using them in the war. You wonder if these pilots know where the Germans are thanks to members of La Dame Blanche.

63

TURN THE PAGE.

You're called to the hospital to treat Germans who've been wounded in the bombing. You gasp as you notice Heinz among the dead.

With Heinz gone, you are no longer a double agent. You work for La Dame Blanche through the end of the war. Years later you proudly tell your children about your days as a spy.

The fierce fighting in World War I created huge numbers of casualties and put nurses and doctors to the test.

THE
-END-

To follow another path, turn to page 11.
To read the conclusion, turn to page 101.

Soon you are trying to get others to support the strike. You and Marthe go to the prison's commander, a mean-looking officer named Berger. You bring up all your courage as you say, "We refuse to do this work anymore!"

Berger looks at you. "You refuse? So, now the prisoners tell me what to do? Guards!" he yells, calling over two men. "Take them away."

You are taken to an even smaller cell than before. Inside the cell there is barely enough room for a hard bed. One tiny window high above you lets in just a sliver of sunlight.

65

You begin feeling sick. Soon your illness gets worse. With Marthe holding your hand, you die, wishing you could see your parents again.

THE
-END-

To follow another path, turn to page 11.
To read the conclusion, turn to page 101.

"I'm just a simple nurse," you say. "I don't know anything about spying."

Heinz doesn't say anything. But his face hardens as he looks at you with sudden distrust. Your heart is beating fast as he walks away.

That evening you visit Mrs. Roenig. You tell her about Colonel Heinz and his request.

"Of course the Germans know about our work," she says. "That is why we must be careful. And if Heinz is suspicious of you, he might have men following you. I think you should stop coming here. Give all your information to Marthe."

You nod, then turn to go. As you step outside, two military police officers step out of the shadows.

"Halt!" one says. "What are you doing out after the curfew?"

"I'm a nurse," you say. "I sometimes take care of Mrs. Roenig."

"Did you know she is suspected of spying for the Allies?" the other officer asks.

"Of course not," you say, but your voice is cracking. The men must know you're lying.

"Come with us," the first officer says. "You're under arrest. Colonel Heinz wants to speak with you."

Your life as a spy is over. You shudder at the thought of spending the rest of the war in a German prison camp.

To follow another path, turn to page 11.
To read the conclusion, turn to page 101.

"A strike will only anger the Germans," you say. "Why make things harder on ourselves?"

Marthe is disappointed, but she sees your point. "Besides," you tell her, "I have an idea. I think I know how we can escape."

You tell Marthe that some of the prisoners are working outside the prison in a nearby town. "We can request to do that work. If they choose us, we can watch carefully—perhaps we'll find a chance to escape." Marthe readily agrees to your plan.

The next week your request is approved. You are handcuffed as you ride in the back of a wagon. The guards free you when you reach the work site. Your new job is helping local farmers harvest their crops. As the day goes on you notice that the guards become lazier. Some nap under a tree. Other talk and laugh, barely paying attention to the prisoners.

The guards seem to pay less attention to you each day. The local people working in the fields ignore you too.

One day you see an opportunity. You nudge Marthe. "Start moving toward those trees. If you're stopped, just say you feel ill and need to rest." Marthe goes and no one notices her. You make the same walk and no one notices you either. The two of you move deeper into the trees, searching for a place to hide.

When night comes you begin to hike through the woods. You move quickly and quietly, knowing if you're discovered the Germans will execute you. **69** Finally, dirty and exhausted, you make it back to Belgium. You've never felt so grateful to be alive.

THE
-END-

To follow another path, turn to page 11.
To read the conclusion, turn to page 101.

Tsar Nicholas II of Russia, just weeks before of World War I.

CHAPTER 4

FIGHTING RUSSIAN REBELS

You live in England, but since the war began you have closely watched events in Russia. Your family once had a business there and lived there for many years. You learned the language, and you still have friends there.

As the war has gone on, you've seen Russia suffer terrible losses. Then, in March 1917 Russian leader Tsar Nicholas II is forced from power. British officials now worry that the new government might stop fighting the Germans. Even when the United States joins the Allies in April 1917, the United Kingdom wants Russia to keep fighting. Russian soldiers in Eastern Europe force Germany to keep troops there, rather than moving them to the Western Front.

71

TURN THE PAGE.

The new Russian government promises to keep fighting. But some members of the government belong to the Communist Party. Many of its members oppose the war. No one in the British government knows what will happen next. They decide it is crucial to send British agents to Russia to gather intelligence.

One day a family friend introduces you to Captain Sir Mansfield Cumming, the head of the Secret Intelligence Service (SIS). You explain your background in Russia and your interest in the events there.

"I know I'm not trained to spy," you say, "but I would like to offer my services."

"We can give you some brief training," Cumming says. "But what's most important is having smart agents who know local people and speak the language. You're just what we need."

You receive training in disguises and message coding. During that time Communists take complete control of Russia under Vladimir Lenin. He meets with German officials and signs a peace treaty. British officials hope to remove the Communists from power and bring Russia back into the war.

In the spring of 1918, you arrive at the British Embassy in Moscow, undercover as a diplomat. Another agent, Allan Hodges, greets you.

"We need information about Lenin and his people," Hodges says. "We also have some troops arriving in northern Russia. We might need them to fight the Communists. They could use someone to gather intelligence. Which would you rather do?"

TO STAY IN MOSCOW, TURN TO PAGE 74.

TO GO NORTH, TURN TO PAGE 80.

Hodges tells you to make contact with Stanley Wilson, another SIS agent. You meet Wilson the next day in a café. He explains what he's been doing.

"I talk to anyone who knows Lenin or knows someone who is close to him," says Wilson. "I've also met with Russians who oppose the Communists."

"Does anyone suspect you work for British intelligence?" you ask.

"I don't think so. I use a code name, of course, and I keep moving from one friend's house to another."

Wilson continues, "There are still plenty of Russians who hate the Communists. And I know one sure way to get rid of the Communists."

You lean closer and say, "Yes?"

"We have to kill Lenin."

You pull back in shock. You thought SIS agents only gathered intelligence. No one said anything to you about an assassination.

"Does Hodges know about this?" you ask.

"I won't say," Wilson replies. "I can tell you that some people in London support the plan. But if the assassination fails and I'm caught, no one will help me. Are you willing to join me?"

You don't like the idea of killing anyone, even a Communist who hates your country. But at the same time, you know how helpful it would be to get rid of the Communist government.

75

TO HELP WILSON, TURN TO PAGE 76.

TO SAY NO, TURN TO PAGE 89.

Wilson takes you to meet a Russian officer named Berkov. He explains the plan as you travel. "Berkov's going to help me. I want to kill Lenin while he's attending an important government meeting. Berkov is arranging to blow up bridges into Moscow so Communist troops can't reach the city. Meanwhile, British and French forces that land in the north will head toward Moscow."

Berkov is excited to get started soon after you arrive. "I have Latvian troops ready to help," he says. "They are sick of Communist rule."

Something about Berkov makes you suspicious. You know that Latvian forces took part in the recent killing of Tsar Nicholas II and his family. They are also key members of the Cheka, the Communist government's secret police. You begin to wonder if Berkov could be a double agent. Is his offer to help really a trick?

Wilson and Berkov continue discussing the details of the plan. After a few minutes, you ask to speak to Wilson alone.

"How well do you know Berkov?" you ask.

"I don't know him that well," Wilson replies. "Do you think he could be a double agent?"

"Exactly," you say.

"I've wondered the same thing. Do you want to report this to Cumming back in London?" Wilson asks. "Or maybe one of us should tail him and see where he leads us."

77

TO SEND A REPORT TO SIS IN LONDON, **TURN TO PAGE 78.**

TO OFFER TO TAIL BERKOV, **TURN TO PAGE 90.**

"I think the SIS should know that the Cheka might be trying to trick us," you say.

You go back out and say goodbye to Berkov. After he leaves Wilson goes back to his apartment and you head to the embassy. You like Wilson but you wonder how skilled he is at spying. His plot to kill Lenin seems almost impossible to carry out. You decide to tell Hodges about the plan and your suspicions of Berkov.

"London needs to know about this," Hodges says. "And I wonder about Wilson sometimes. He takes risks a good spy shouldn't take. You seem much more careful."

It's nice to hear Hodges speak well of you, especially since you are so new to espionage.

The next day, as you're about to head out to meet one of your contacts, you see Hodges. "I just spoke with Wilson," he says. "He denies working with Berkov on a plot. But I trust you. I'm sending Wilson back to London. As for you, I need a good man to head north on a special assignment. Will you go?"

You agree, glad that Hodges trusts you and your talents.

Vladimir Lenin angered the Allies when his new government made peace with Germany and began withdrawing Russian troops from the front.

TURN THE PAGE.

You begin a voyage by sea to the city of Archangel. Allied ships had used the port there to bring supplies to the Russians. But Russia is now in the middle of a civil war between the Communists and other Russians who oppose them. Now the ships deliver Allied troops to help fight the Communists. Getting into the port is dangerous. German submarines called U-boats patrol below the water's surface. You breathe a sigh of relief when you're safely off the ship.

In Archangel you grow a beard and start to dress as a Russian. You tell people you are a businessman named Ivan Forenko. You try to meet Russians who will help you against the Communists, but you don't have much luck.

One day you receive a coded message from London: "Go to Petrograd. Gather information about Russian forces and attitude of the people."

You travel by train to Petrograd. Until recently it was Russia's capital. A naval officer named Cromie was in charge of gathering intelligence there for the British, but he was recently killed by a mob. Your mission is to find his contacts and continue his work. You have one name—an English businessman named Taylor. But when you go to his house, you learn he has been arrested. You worry that if anyone learns you're not really Russian, you'll be arrested too.

On the street a man approaches you. He asks in Russian if you were looking for Taylor. You're surprised by the question, then answer yes.

"Don't worry," he says. "I worked with him. If you are a friend of his, then I will help you."

"Yes, I was looking for him," you say. "He and I are in the same business."

TURN THE PAGE.

"Ah, good, I hoped so," the man says. "My name is Stefan Korovich. The Communists killed my parents after the revolution. That is why I helped Taylor. And now I can help you. Come with me and I'll find you a place to sleep tonight."

Something seems odd. How did Korovich know you were looking for Taylor? He could be a double agent working for the Communists. But if he is really on your side, he could be of great help.

Allied troops encountered brutal winter weather in Russia as they fought the Communists.

TO GO WITH KOROVICH, GO TO PAGE 83.

TO REFUSE TO GO, TURN TO PAGE 85.

You follow Korovich as he leads you down the street to a café. He tells the woman there to bring you food. The war and revolution have severely damaged Russia. Many people beg for food on the streets. But the woman gives you fresh bread and fish.

Korovich tells you that few people go to Taylor's building. "I question each one I see," he says. "You are the first one who knows about his espionage." Korovich says he can put you in contact with people who have information about the Communists' war plans.

"It is horrible now," Korovich says. "Cheka agents arrest anyone they think is not a devoted Communist. Sometimes the people are killed."

TURN THE PAGE.

"Do you think they will kill Taylor?" you ask.

"Probably. And his wife too."

You didn't realize Taylor was married. And you're angry that the Communists would kill his wife.

"Is there anything we can do to free her?" you ask.

"I know a police officer at the jail where she is kept," Korovich says. "If we offer enough money, he might help her escape. And you will have to bribe others to get her out of Russia."

84

Paying bribes and arranging escapes was not what you were sent here to do. Perhaps you should forget about helping Mrs. Taylor. But how can you let an innocent woman die?

TO PLAN THE ESCAPE,
TURN TO PAGE 92.

TO FORGET THE IDEA,
TURN TO PAGE 94.

"I don't know what you think I meant," you say. "Taylor and I work together sending Russian goods overseas. Thank you anyway."

You turn and walk away. The man calls after you, but you ignore him.

With Taylor arrested you realize you have to get contacts on your own. You have one more lead. In Archangel you heard about a private café where men who oppose the Communists sometimes gather. You make plans to find it tomorrow. In the meantime you rent a room.

The next day you walk across the city to the café. The door is locked. You knock and someone comes to the door but does not open it.

85

"Who's there?" the voice asks.

"Taylor sent me," you say. "And I was a friend of Cromie's." After a moment he opens the door.

TURN THE PAGE.

Several men are sitting around a table drinking coffee—and one of them is Korovich.

"I knew you were one of us," he says, smiling. He introduces you to the others. You ask them the best way to find out about the Communists' military units and their strategy for the war.

"You could join the Communists in the Red Army," one man said with a laugh.

"That may not be a bad idea," Korovich says. "You wouldn't be stopped on the street, like the Cheka does to us now. No one would suspect you of anything. But you would have to play the role of a faithful Communist."

86

You're already pretending to be someone you're not, but you won't be much use as a spy if you get killed in battle.

TO JOIN THE RED ARMY,
GO TO PAGE 87.

TO DO OTHER SPY WORK,
TURN TO PAGE 96.

Korovich helps arrange for you to volunteer with a Red Army unit just outside Petrograd. You quickly learn one advantage of being a soldier—you receive more food than civilians do. But you quickly learn that most of the soldiers are not loyal Communists.

"We would leave today, if we could," says a soldier named Pretrov. "But if we desert, they will throw all of our relatives into prison camps. And we hear they keep loyal troops in the rear to shoot anyone who tries to desert."

You serve as an assistant to an officer. Like many of the other soldiers, he does not want to be fighting other Russians in the civil war. But he knows he cannot desert. "I will just follow orders and hope that the Allies can help the White Army win." He uses the common name for the army battling the Communists.

You have a great deal of freedom in the army and continue to meet with Korovich. One day, though, you hear that your unit is heading off to battle far from Petrograd. If you go it will be harder for you to send any information back to London. You think about deserting.

Fighting between the Red Army and White Army went on for several years after the end of World War I. The Red Army eventually won the Russian Civil War.

TO DESERT,
TURN TO PAGE 98.

TO STAY IN THE ARMY,
TURN TO PAGE 99.

Wilson asks you to keep quiet about the plan. For the next few weeks, you search for Russians who oppose the Communists. On August 30 you're at the embassy when a man rushes in, yelling, "Someone has shot Vladimir Lenin! He was wounded but is still alive!"

After learning that the shooting took place outside a factory, you run to see Hodges. He claims not to know anything about the attack.

The next day Cheka agents arrest Hodges, claiming the embassy directed the shooting.

The next day an angry crowd storms the British Embassy in Petrograd. Life as a spy is becoming too dangerous for you. You send a message to London and ask to come home.

89

THE -END-

To follow another path, turn to page 11.
To read the conclusion, turn to page 101.

"I'll tail him," you say.

You and Wilson go back out to Berkov. Wilson explains that you have to leave. You rush back to the embassy. There you put on the clothes of a Russian peasant and paste a false moustache above your lip. Then you race back to the café so you can wait for Berkov to leave.

After a few minutes, he walks out into the street. You move behind him, staying about one hundred feet back. He slips into an office building. You wait for him to come out. When he does another man is with him. You recognize Berkov's companion—he's a member of the Cheka! You begin to follow them, but suddenly two large men step into your path.

"Come with us," one of them says. "We know you work for the British Embassy. But why would a diplomat be creeping around in disguise at the Cheka office?"

You decide it's better not to answer. You need to tell Hodges about the Cheka's attempt to sabotage Wilson's plot. But your heart sinks when the men lock you in a dank, windowless cell. Something tells you they won't be releasing you anytime soon.

Members of the Cheka could search, arrest, and interrogate civilians in their search for enemies of the state.

THE
-END-

To follow another path, turn to page 11.
To read the conclusion, turn to page 101.

You give Korovich all the money you have to use as a bribe. Then you message London, asking SIS to send more money. Over the next few days, Korovich helps you arrange all the other bribes. Finally, the night comes for the escape.

"The officer will leave a green shawl in the ladies' room," Korovich says." He will bring her in, then let her find the shawl. Wrapped up in it will be a pass that allows her to leave the jail."

That night you wait nervously outside the jail. If something goes wrong, the Cheka will surely kill Mrs. Taylor. But as snow falls, you see a woman with a green shawl leave the building. You rush over to her and explain who you are.

"Thank you for taking this risk for me," Mrs. Taylor says, beginning to cry.

Korovich explains the plan for getting you and Mrs. Taylor into neighboring Finland.

After several hours on a train, you meet your first contact, a Finn named Sitta. He takes you through the forests on a horse-drawn sled. You are nearing the border when you see a dark figure.

As the sled pulls up beside the man, you worry that he might be a Communist soldier. Sitta speaks to the man in Finnish.

"It's all right," Sitta tells you. "He just wanted to warn us to take a different path."

As morning comes, Sitta takes you over the border. Another man will now help Mrs. Taylor reach England. And you will return to your spying duties. You smile to yourself. No matter what else happens, at least you were able to help one person escape a bad situation.

THE
-END-

To follow another path, turn to page 11.
To read the conclusion, turn to page 101.

"I can't take such a big risk," you tell Korovich. He seems to understand.

You finish eating and Korovich takes you to a small apartment he owns nearby. You see the bed and head for it, exhausted after your travels.

"Meet me tomorrow," he tells you, handing you an address. "I want you to meet others who support our cause against the Communists."

When the morning comes, you look at yourself in the mirror. With your beard and hair getting longer, you barely recognize yourself. And you haven't spoken English to anyone in days.

"Well, no one ever said spying would be easy," you say in English. You remember that you are doing this to help your country and to fight Communism. Lenin and his supporters have said they want to spread their style of government around the world.

You dress and head to the restaurant. After a few minutes, you see Korovich with two other men. They come and sit at your table. Just as Korovich begins to introduce them, a dozen soldiers rush into the restaurant.

"Run!" Korovich yells, as he and the other men bolt from the table. They don't get far before the soldiers surround them, their guns ready to fire. One of the soldiers comes to grab you too.

"They must have followed me here," Korovich hisses. "The Cheka must know about me."

"Shut up!" a soldier says, jabbing Korovich with his gun. The soldiers march you and the other three men out. You are headed to prison and you will be lucky to get out alive.

THE
–END–

To follow another path, turn to page 11.
To read the conclusion, turn to page 101.

Korovich understands your desire to stay in Petrograd. And he and the others with him will do everything they can to help.

You spend as much time as you can along the city's docks, watching the Russian navy ships. You note when ships come and go in your messages back to London.

After a few months you think you are being followed. The SIS wants you to leave Russia before you're arrested. You receive a coded message to go to the docks. The British navy is sending a small, fast boat to bring you to Finland.

Korovich helps arrange for someone to row you into the harbor. The British boat will pick you up there—if it can get past Russian boats that patrol the waters. In addition the Russians have a fort on an island in the harbor.

You and Korovich's friend row your boat as quietly as possible. Soon, you see searchlights coming from the fort. They must be looking for the British boat! Somehow, the captain moves the small craft so that it avoids the wide beams of light. The boat pulls up next to yours and you board. You collapse in the boat, exhausted. You hope you will make it to Finland safely.

Communist patrols would have been suspicious of foreigners. Spies had to carefully blend in with civilians.

THE
−END−

To follow another path, turn to page 11.
To read the conclusion, turn to page 101.

That night, you head to the rear of the camp. Knowing that troops have orders to shoot deserters, you keep low and walk quietly.

You are almost at the edge of camp when you hear some shouts and a gunshot. You stay low and move in a zigzag. A few more shots ring out, but then everything is quiet.

Hours later, you reach Petrograd. You find Korovich in the private café. He arranges for you to get civilian clothes. By trimming your hair and beard differently and putting on a large fur hat, you create another disguise.

He suggests you leave Russia by taking a train to the border with Latvia. You realize how much you miss England. It will be good to return home.

THE -END-

To follow another path, turn to page 11.
To read the conclusion, turn to page 101.

Your unit boards northbound trains. You realize you could end up fighting the British. The war in Europe is now over, but the Allies still want to end Communist rule in Russia.

As you travel north, the winter weather gets worse and worse. You hear that some nights, the temperature falls to minus 50 degrees Fahrenheit.

When you reach a small town, the train stops. The Red Army has orders to drive out nearby American troops. You decide that you will try to desert and reach the Americans.

You try to stay in the rear and avoid the firing. But the American artillery shells are starting to land closer to you. You turn to run, but in a second, a shell explodes and kills you instantly.

THE
–END–

To follow another path, turn to page 11.
To read the conclusion, turn to page 101.

MORE BRITISH GAINS—NEW FOE PEACE OFFER

The Daily Mirror

CERTIFIED CIRCULATION LARGER THAN THAT OF ANY OTHER DAILY PICTURE PAPER

No. 4,195. Registered at the G.P.O. as a Newspaper. WEDNESDAY, APRIL 4, 1917. One Penny.

U.S.A. DECLARE A STATE OF WAR WITH GERMANY—AMERICANS WHO HAVE FOUGHT AND BLED FOR THE ALLIES.

President Wilson (wearing tall-hat) at a review of troops.

The North Atlantic fleet steaming in line of battle.

Three Americans, now in the British Army, who have all been wounded. In the centre is Private O'Connor, formerly a missionary.

Marines take part in a sham battle at manœuvres. The "wounded" have fallen down.

German liners which have been interned since the beginning of the war in dock at Hoboken, New Jersey.

While President Wilson was delivering his great indictment of Hohenzollernism before Congress came the news that the American armed liner Aztec had been torpedoed. There were scenes of remarkable enthusiasm after the speech, the members waving handkerchiefs and flags and raising deafening cheers. One of the first acts expected is the seizure of the German and Austrian ships in American ports. They number eighty, including the huge liner Vaterland.

The United States entered World War I in 1917, declaring war on Germany and its allies on April 6.

CHAPTER 5

SPYING IN THE GREAT WAR AND BEYOND

Europe's Great War would later be called World War I, after a second world war began in 1939. During World War I, both sides used spies, counterespionage, and secret codes. World War I ended in November 1918 with an Allied victory over Germany and its allies.

Espionage played a part in the United States' late entry into the war. British agents had broken codes Germany used to send secret messages. Hoping to gain useful information, they eventually intercepted a message that helped convince the United States to join the fight.

In January 1917 German diplomat Arthur Zimmerman sent a message to another diplomat. The message outlined a plan to ask Mexico to join the war and take Germany's side. The Germans had agreed to give Mexico some U.S. land that had once been part of Mexico. British agents passed the message on to the United States. This scheme, along with German attacks on American ships, led President Woodrow Wilson to declare war against Germany.

After entering the war, the United States sent some spies to Mexico to see if the Germans were active there. The Federal Bureau of Investigation (FBI) also played a part in espionage. After the war the U.S. navy and army increased their intelligence gathering efforts. But European countries were more involved in spying during the war.

The Russian Communists won their war against the Allies and the White Army in 1920. American suspicions of the Communists led to decades of espionage between the two countries.

TELEGRAM RECEIVED.

FROM 2nd from London # 5747.

"We intend to begin on the first of February unrestricted submarine warfare. We shall endeavor in spite of this to keep the United States of America neutral. In the event of this not succeeding, we make Mexico a proposal of alliance on the following basis: make war together, make peace together, generous financial support and an understanding on our part that Mexico is to reconquer the lost territory in Texas, New Mexico, and Arizona. The settlement in detail is left to you. You will inform the President of the above most secretly as soon as the outbreak of war with the United States of America is certain and add the suggestion that he should, on his own initiative, invite Japan to immediate adherence and at the same time mediate between Japan and ourselves. Please call the President's attention to the fact that the ruthless employment of our submarines now offers the prospect of compelling England in a few months to make peace." Signed, ZIMMERMANN.

The Zimmerman telegram had a huge effect on public opinion in the United States. It caused many Americans to support their country entering the war.

Today, the Central Intelligence Agency (CIA) is the main American agency for collecting intelligence overseas. And the FBI still searches for foreign spies in the United States. The National Security Agency (NSA) secretly gathers information electronically from around the world. In the United Kingdom, the SIS is now called MI6. The Security Service, now called MI5, still conducts counterespionage.

Other countries have developed their spy networks as well, sometimes spying on allies as well as enemies. Technology such as spy satellites allows countries to watch another nation's military actions. Computers help agents break codes and store information they gather electronically. Countries also try to steal information by hacking, or breaking into, computer networks.

Despite modern technology many agents around the world still use traditional methods of espionage. They enter foreign countries, use false names, and gather information, just as spies did during World War I.

Airplanes were a new invention that both sides tried to use for espionage during the war. Low-flying planes provided valuable intelligence about enemy numbers, strength, and locations.

1909—The United Kingdom creates the Secret Service Bureau, which later includes the Security Service and the Secret Intelligence Service.

JUNE 28, 1914—Franz Ferdinand of Austria-Hungary is assassinated in Sarajevo.

JULY 28, 1914—Austria-Hungary declares war on Serbia, and each side's allies soon follow.

AUGUST 4, 1914—Germany invades Belgium and controls parts of it throughout the war.

NOVEMBER 6, 1914—The British execute Carl Lody for spying for Germany.

1915—German agents try but fail to blow up the Welland Canal in Ontario, Canada.

1916—Belgians create La Dame Blanche.

JULY 30, 1916—German agents blow up munitions at Black Tom Island, New York.

JANUARY 11, 1917—German agents blow up a munitions factory in Kingsland, New Jersey.

FEBRUARY 1917—President Woodrow Wilson learns about Germany's secret effort to recruit Mexico to fight the United States.

APRIL 6, 1917—The United States declares war on Germany.

NOVEMBER 1917—Communists take control of Russia's government.

MARCH 3, 1918—Russia signs a peace treaty with the Central Powers.

AUGUST 1918—Allied forces take control of Archangel.

NOVEMBER 11, 1918—World War I ends.

1919—Allied troops support Russia's White Army against the Communists.

NOVEMBER 1920—Communists defeat the White Army in the Russian Civil War.

OTHER PATHS
TO EXPLORE

In this book, you've seen how events from the past look different from three points of view. Perspectives on history are as varied as the people who lived it. Seeing history from many points of view is an important part of understanding it. Here are ideas for other World War I espionage points of view to explore:

+ Many scientists, historians, and other types of academics were asked to spy while doing their research. Do you think it is ethical for scholars to use their position as a cover for doing espionage? Why or why not? Support your answer with examples from at least two other texts or valid Internet sources.
(Integration of Knowledge and Ideas)

+ Nineteen-year-old Gavrilo Princip fired the shots that killed Austrian Archduke Franz Ferdinand and his wife Sophie and sparked World War I. What factors led Princip to become an assassin? What did he hope to accomplish? Support your answers using information from at least two other texts or valid Internet sources.
(Key Ideas and Details)

READ MORE

Bearce, Stephanie. *Top Secret Files: World War I Spies, Secret Missions, & Hidden Facts from World War I.* Waco, Tex.: Prufrock Press, 2015.

George, Enzo. *World War I: The War to End All Wars.* New York: Cavendish Square, 2015.

Mitchell, Susan K. *The Secret World of Spy Agencies.* Berkeley Heights, N.J.: Enslow Publishers, 2012.

Price, Sean. *Modern Spies.* North Mankato, Minn.: Capstone Press, 2014.

INTERNET SITES

FactHound offers a safe, fun way to find Internet sites related to this book. All of the sites on FactHound have been researched by our staff.

Here's all you do:
Visit *www.facthound.com*
Type in this code: 9781491458600

GLOSSARY

assassination (uh-sass-uh-NAY-shun)—the murder of someone who is well known or important

bribe (BRIBE)—money or gifts used to persuade someone to do something; especially something illegal or dishonest

Communist (KAHM-yuh-nist)—a person who believes in a system in which goods and property are owned by the government and shared in common

counterespionage (koun-tur-ESS-pee-uh-nahzh)—the efforts of one country to catch foreign spies; to prevent or stop enemies from spying

desert (di-ZUHRT)—to leave military service without permission

diplomat (DI-pluh-mat)—someone who deals with other nations to create or maintain good relationships

embassy (EM-buh-see)—a building where representatives from another country work

fluent (FLOO-uhnt)—able to easily speak a language

munitions (myoo-NIH-shuhns)—materials used to wage war, including ammunition and weapons

sabotage (SAB-uh-tahzh)—damage or destruction of property that is done on purpose

BIBLIOGRAPHY

Andrew, Christopher M. *The Sword and the Shield: The Mitrokhin Archive and the Secret History of the KGB.* New York: Basic Books, 1999.

Blum, Howard. *Dark Invasion: 1915: Germany's Secret War and the Hunt for the First Terrorist Cell in America.* New York: Harper, 2014.

Dukes, Paul. *Red Dusk and the Morrow: Adventures and Investigations in Soviet Russia.* London: Biteback Publishing, 2012.

Jeffrey, Keith. *The Secret History of MI6.* New York: Penguin Press, 2010.

Landau, Henry. *The Enemy Within; The Inside Story of German Sabotage in America.* New York: G. P. Putnam's Sons, 1937.

Macrakis, Kristie. *Prisoners, Lovers, & Spies: The Story of Invisible Ink from Herodotus to al-Qaeda.* New Haven: Yale University Press, 2014.

McKenna, Marthe Cnokaert. *I Was a Spy!* New York: R. M. McBride & Company, 1933.

Proctor, Tammy M. *Female Intelligence: Women and Espionage in the First World War.* New York: New York University, 2003.

INDEX